MW01102587

SWOT WORKBOOK

Updated

February 18, 2019

BY Julia A Fox

Failing Forward 2nd Edition

SWOT WORKBOOK

This Workbook works with the book

Failing Forward 2nd Edition - Don't Give Up

This is an exercise that will help you identify all the areas in your life that you think you need to change. Some of those areas won't even present themselves to you until you go through the workbook.

Since the personal growth you will obtain from doing this workbook will help you achieve more things in your life than you can possibly imagine. I personally have done this exercise 11 times.

The reason is... where you are right now is not where you're going to be in six months if you work this program. What you will achieve is a comfort level with yourself that you never thought was even possible. Food for thought: write the date of each of your entries. Go back a few weeks later and look at what you wrote.

Do your SWOT again after about 6 months. You will be amazed at what has changed and what hasn't.

This is what I did, and I actually got to watch myself grow and change! Its an awesome feeling to see how much I accomplished in a short time. It takes commitment though! Things will change! They always do, its up to you which direction your life changes.

What I gained from doing this exercise so many times was learning who I was as a person now as opposed to where I was before. Believe me its better now!

So many times, my clients tell me

"I just want to be happy".

This workbook will help you get started on the path to learning you and being happy! I was never good at saying no or setting boundaries with people without feeling really guilty anyway. Now I can.

This has helped me in all areas of my life, and a lot of areas I didn't even recognize at first. You can do this!

And don't forget –

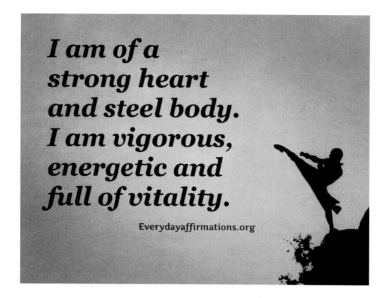

You Are Important!

SWOT =

- Strengths
- Weaknesses
- Opportunities
- Threats

I am so excited for you! The book gives you a much more in-depth view of the overall process to healing.

Using this model will really help you build some Self-esteem and Heal!

No More Walking on Eggshells!

This exercise is so motivating because you will learn so much about yourself that you didn't even realize. You will be able to identify areas that you are awesome at and areas that you need to work on.

You will literally clear the "fog" out of your mind and be able to see clearly, maybe for the first time in many years.
You are important! Don't give up!

I developed this exercise to help me figure out how I could make myself "Feel" better… It worked!

I am not going to lie… it takes work to get to where you want to be! This is more than work though… Its life changing! This workbook changed my life forever! Now I can look in the mirror and go "Yep I really like you"!

> How can I go forward when
> I don't know which way
> I'm facing?
>
> —John Lennon

STRENGTHS

- Write down all of your strengths. Strength can be anything you believe you're good at. For example: I am really good at growing plants.

The first time I did this exercise I couldn't think of anything that I was really good at, so I called people that I trusted and asked. I was surprised at some of the answers that I received.

Write down everything that you can think of and then, call other people like I did you might be surprised!

Take notes when you are talking to your people. This part was really good for me because I didn't believe in myself right then. I do now though, and you will to!

EXAMPLE:

1. I AM STRONG BECAUSE I AM DOING EVERYTHING I CAN TO TAKE CARE OF MYSELF.

AND I DON'T FEEL GUILTY ABOUT IT EITHER!

Start here!

I am strong because…. One of my strengths are….

Todays date:

_____

_____

_____

_____

_____

_____

_____

_____

WEAKNESSES

this part of the exercise was really easy for me because I could think of everything that I did wrong and why I thought it was week. For example, my biggest weakness was that I couldn't tell people no.

Another weakness I had was that I felt guilty about everything. I learned exactly who my friends were back then. Most of the people that were around me are basically sucking the life force energy out of me. They are what are known as "emotional vampires".

This part of the exercise will help you learn what it is that you need to work on at this particular moment. At first, I was really discouraged because what I saw was only fault in myself.

But what I actually learned was how to set up my own boundaries and how to make my life more user-friendly for me. You can do this!

You Are Important! Don't Give Up!

WEAKNESSES

While thinking about this, please do not beat yourself up by pointing out what you believe are your faults. This part is only to find areas that you believe you need to work on. The action of writing just one thing down will help you think of other things. Do not get discouraged. You can do this!

Weaknesses do not inherently say that you a weak. They are simply things that that you will come to recognize as areas to work on that will help you become the person that you want to be…I needed to work on saying "No" to people who continuously need me to fix their problems because I have my own life to live (drama free). Sometimes you just cannot help them the way they want to be helped! That is not your problem!

I Do Not Feel Guilty!

Today is a brand new day.
My past does not define me.
My future is mine to create.

PersonalExcellence.co

OPPORTUNITIES

This section was hard for me because I felt trapped with no way out. However, you are making opportunities for yourself because you are working and doing everything you can to learn "how to" make positive changes in your life just by doing this module.

There are programs out there in your community that can help you. There are programs to get clothes, to teach you new skills so you can get a job and help you go to school. There are programs for daycare if you have small children. There are programs that provide free counseling which I have utilized myself.

Sometimes you must look really hard for the programs. Keep asking questions until you get the answers you need.

An opportunity may be the ability to find the help you need for housing, food or a job. Catholic Charities is a good place to start!

In the United States, programs such as the YWCA provide free domestic violence counseling.

Goodwill has its own employment security Department and they will help you find a job, Catholic Charities provides counseling and work programs with clothes. There re programs for housing too.

These programs will lead you to even more programs and soon you will have built your own support system. Keep asking questions until you get the answers you are looking for! There's a saying "the squeaky wheel gets the grease" … dig deep and keep asking questions!

What Opportunities do you think are available to you or that you can create?

I have the
power to
create change.
IΔMRUBY

_____

_____

_____

_____

_____

_____

_____

_____

_____

_____

_____

_____

THREATS

When the world seems really big it can be quite overwhelming. Give yourself 5 minutes to breathe deeply to get your mind relaxed enough so you can write a list. Taking that first step in your own self-care is one of the biggest steps you will ever take. The biggest threat that any of us have had to deal with is fear. I used to be afraid of everything. Today, I know I can overcome anything. As you can too!

A threat could be some of those people that have been using you up and requiring that you spend all your time and energy on their problems. I personally have had to let go of a lot of people and things. Letting go of people that you love or things you love will feel uncomfortable to say the least at first. In my journey, I learned that most of those people were definitely not my friends and I got more stuff!

A threat is someone who was holding you back from being who you want to be. I had to learn to love people from a distance so-to-speak. Letting go of people that were dragging me down and putting me in situations not good for me was the best thing that I ever learned how to do. It was hard at first, but after a while a huge weight was lifted off me. And I could breathe!

Write down some of the threats that you can think of and take your time because once you start identifying things; this will answer a lot more questions for you.

Bed Time Affirmations for the Soul:
- I have done my Best for today.
- I have earned my Rest for tonight.
- I have put my Love into all my deeds.
- I have used Kindness in all my thoughts.
- I close this day with pure Joy
and now drift into a Sound Sleep.

Good Night

Think Positive Words

Our actions and decisions today will shape the way we will be living in the future.

THREATS

A threat may be that you have a really hard time saying no to people. I covered this in the weaknesses section also. We must look at our part in the situation also. Be accountable to yourself.

I'm not saying anything is your fault by any means. I'm just saying that we must be accountable to ourselves. As hard as that may sound it's so true.

Another threat may be that you do not make time to take care of yourself. 5 minutes helps however, 30 minutes or more is better. What is in your life that you would like to change so that you can feel better about you? What or who is holding you back? How can you help yourself?

_____

_____

In conclusion,

It is very likely that you will have many obstacles to overcome. I'm here to tell you that you can do that. Where there's a will there's a way. Don't Give Up!

I know you are probably worn out with everything and exhausted. Make time for yourself so that you can recharge. You can spend a half an hour in the bathtub with bubbles and candles.

The biggest thing that I learned was that I was my only true threat! Instead of saying I can't do this anymore. I started saying, I'm not doing that anymore.

Doing this workbook will help you redefine your own boundaries, and you will be able to stick with it.

If I can do it – so can you!

Periodically go back and read what you wrote throughout the book and see what's changed. Do the exercises again and really see what's changed! You will be amazed at how strong and awesome you are now! Love yourself first that way you have love to give. It is impossible to give anything when your cup is empty, and you are out of gas. More room to write ideas!

DEVELOPGOODHABITS.COM

<u>"Failing Forward 2nd Edition</u>

Don't Give Up"

I AM SO VERY PROUD OF YOU!

What have you learned about yourself? What areas can you work on to make things better for yourself? You are so awesome taking this first step, it's a hard one but you've done it and I'm so proud of you! Now anything is possible!

You've earned your own self-respect! You are on your way to changing your world into whatever you want it to be! You are allowed to be happy regardless of other people and situations.

Certificate of Appreciation

This certificate is awarded to

in recognition of valuable contributions to

To Yourself! Great Job!

Your signature

Date

Julia A Fox

Julia A Fox

Date

Made in the USA
Middletown, DE
15 January 2020

83184305R00027